W9-BVU-356

SUGAR GROVE PUBLIC LIBRARY DISTRICT
54 Snow Street / P.O. Box 1049
Sugar Grove, IL 60554
(630) 466-4686

10/17/06

www.sugargrove.lib.il.us

SUGAR GROVE PUBLIC LIBRARY DISTRICT
54 Snow Street/P.O. Box 1049
Sugar Grove, IL 60554
(630) 466-4686

Fact Finders®

Explore the Biomes

EXPLORE THE

Grasslands

by Kay Jackson

Consultant:
Dr. Sandra Mather
Professor Emerita of Geology and Astronomy
West Chester University
West Chester, Pennsylvania

Capstone press®
Mankato, Minnesota

Fact Finders is published by Capstone Press,
151 Good Counsel Drive, P.O. Box 669, Mankato, Minnesota 56002.
www.capstonepress.com

Library of Congress Cataloging-in-Publication Data
Jackson, Kay, 1959–
    Explore the grasslands / by Kay Jackson.
        p. cm. —(Fact finders. Explore the biomes)
    Includes bibliographical references and index.
    ISBN-13: 978-0-7368-6405-3 (hardcover)
    ISBN-10: 0-7368-6405-9 (hardcover)
    ISBN-13: 978-0-7368-7508-0 (softcover pbk.)
    ISBN-10: 0-7368-7508-5 (softcover pbk.)
    1. Grassland ecology—Juvenile literature. I. Title. II. Series.
QH541.5.P7J33 2007
577.4—dc22   2006005641

Summary: Discusses the plants, animals, and characteristics of the grasslands biome.

Editorial Credits

Erika L. Shores, editor; Juliette Peters, designer; Tami Collins, map illustrator;
    Wanda Winch, photo researcher

Photo Credits

Allen Blake Sheldon, 12–13
Corbis/Paul A. Souders, 6; M. ou Me. Desjeux, Bernard, 22–23
Courtesy of Kay Jackson, 32
Image courtesy of Con Slobodchikoff, 29 (inset)
The Image Works/Jenny Hager, 17; Sean Sprague, 9, 21
James P. Rowan, backcover, 8–9, 10 (grasshopper), 14, 27 (tree)
Minden Pictures/Jim Brandenburg, cover (background), 18–19, 29; Mitsuaki Iwago, 15
Photo by Kansas Scenic Byways Program, 24
Photodisc, 3; Siede Preis, back cover
Shutterstock/Brad Thompson, 4 (hawk); Darko Novakovic, 16 (tree); EcoPrint, 15 (lion); Geir
    Olva Lyngfjell, 21 (child); JG Swanepoel, 6 (impala); Keith Levit, 27 (lion); Lyle E. Doberstein,
    11; Michael Rolands, 1, 30 (wildflower), 25 (flower); Peter Hanson, cover (foreground);
    SF Photography, 14 (gazelle)
Steve Mulligan, 4–5, 19 (grass)
Tom Bean, 25

1 2 3 4 5 6 11 10 09 08 07 06

Table of Contents

CHAPTER 1

A Sea of Grass

Blades and stems rustle. Colorful wildflowers dot the land. Deer graze and hawks soar overhead. A gust of wind ripples like a wave over a sea of grass, the grasslands.

Grasslands lie on the flat land or rolling hills between forests and deserts. Grasses grow where it is too dry for trees but too wet for cactuses. Some bushes grow here, but few trees can live in grassland soil.

red-tailed hawk

Wildflowers and grasses stretch as far as the eye can see on the grasslands.

The Grasslands Biome

Grasslands are one of the world's **biomes**. A biome is a large area where plants and animals have adapted to life in a certain **climate**. Living things in a biome depend on each other. Many animals eat grassland plants. In turn, larger animals survive by eating the grass-eating animals. When animals and plants die, they feed the soil so new plants can grow.

impala

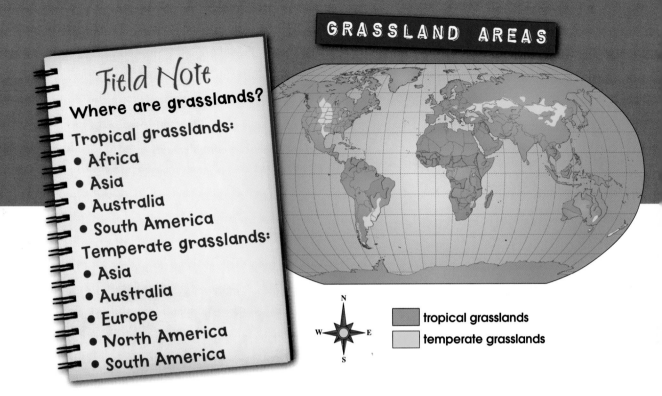

Field Note

Where are grasslands?

Tropical grasslands:
- Africa
- Asia
- Australia
- South America

Temperate grasslands:
- Asia
- Australia
- Europe
- North America
- South America

N W E S

☐ tropical grasslands
☐ temperate grasslands

Different types of grasslands grow in different climates. Tropical grasslands are called savannas. Savannas are warm all year. They have a hot, dry season and a cooler, wet one. Temperate grasslands are called prairies or steppes. In winter, snow whips across these open spaces. Summers are short but hot. Seasons on the prairie bring many changes.

Prairie Seasons

During spring, a soft, green blanket of grass covers prairie hills. Short sprigs of grama grass grow longer as the soil warms. As the days get longer and hotter, wildflowers push up through the prairie soil.

Prairie flowers bloom in early summer. Skyrockets' thin red bells swing in the wind. Soft yellow black-eyed susans catch the morning dew. Purple spikes of blazing star wildflowers poke out above the grass.

Blazing star wildflowers color a prairie with their bright purple flowers.

By fall, colorful flowers wither, leaving behind brown seeds. Round orange and red berries hang from the bare branches of bushes. Tall green grasses dry into straw.

Soon, winter snow falls on the prairie, covering grasses and flowers. Small animals that fly, hop, and slide among their stems will wait for spring to return to the prairie.

Field Note

Black-eyed susans:

- grow 3 feet (91 centimeters) tall
- black-brown centers
- yellow petals
- green leaves about 3 inches (8 centimeters) long

CHAPTER 2

Grassland Animals

Animals fill grasslands with humming, buzzing, and crunching sounds. Over the swishing of the grass, the hum of buzzing bees is heard. They fly from flower to flower, sipping sweet **nectar** from the blossoms. The bees return to a hive where the nectar is made into honey.

Brown and green grasshoppers hang on thin stems. The hungry insects munch on juicy grass blades. Some years, giant swarms of grasshoppers crawl and hop over the grasslands. They chomp through entire fields, leaving behind only short stubs of grass.

grasshopper

Pollen from a thistle rubs off on a bumblebee's body.

FACT!

Honeybees talk by dancing. If a bee finds a wildflower field, it flies back to the hive and does a dance. Its wiggles and turns tell the other bees where to find the field.

A milk snake quietly slides between clumps of grass and wildflowers. A striped skink lizard dashes out. It doesn't see the snake hiding in the grass. Snap! The snake's strong jaws snatch up a meal.

Other hunters aren't as lucky. Every day, the dangerous game between **predator** and **prey** goes on across the grasslands.

Field Note

Milk snake:

- 24 to 52 inches (61 to 132 centimeters) long

- light gray or brown with rusty red spots on body

- eats rodents and reptiles

A milk snake swallows a skink lizard whole.

Grazers and Hunters

Africa's grasslands stretch for miles between dry deserts and thick, green rain forests. On these savannas, herds of zebras, antelope, and gazelles graze on tall grasses. Their teeth snip off the tops of the blades.

Grant's gazelle

African lion

Hungry lions hide in the grass, watching the herds pass by. A young zebra stops for a nibble. A lion bursts into a run after the grazer. Their chase zigzags through the herds. The zebra outruns the lion this time. But one day, the lion's sharp claws and teeth will catch its meal.

A zebra's best defense against attacking predators is its speed.

CHAPTER 3

Grasses Fight for Space

At the edge of the grasslands, a war is taking place. Trees and bushes try to take over the grasses' land. Grasses fight to keep their home.

A tall oak tree towers over prairie grass. Underneath the tree, grass can't grow in the dark shade. Over time, trees can spread on the prairie and keep grass from growing.

Grasses have their own ways to fight back. Roots are grasses' secret weapons. The thick, tangled mat of grass roots survives even if the grass is eaten or killed in freezing weather. Young tree saplings, however, die if they freeze or are eaten.

oak tree

The long roots of grasses grow deep into the soil.

FACT!

The roots of the black walnut tree keep grasses away. Their roots release a poison that kills grasses and other trees.

Fire on Grasslands

A bolt of lightning strikes the ground. A thunder storm rolls over the grasslands. Strong winds blow. But the storm passes without any rain falling. The dry season has come to the grasslands.

Where the lightning struck, a puff of smoke rises in the air. Orange flames begin to spread fire across the land, burning it to a blackened crisp.

Huge fires spread quickly across dry grasslands.

The fire kills everything in its path. But grass roots underground stay alive. They'll sprout again when the rain returns. As long as fires burn each year, trees and bushes don't have a chance to grow on the grasslands.

Not long after a fire burns the prairie, new grass pushes up from the earth.

19

CHAPTER 4

People and Grasslands

The Maasai people live on the savannas in Kenya. The Maasai get everything they need from the cattle, sheep, and goats they raise. The animals are used for milk, meat, and clothes.

The Maasai are nomads. If a place doesn't have enough grass or water, they move with their herds to a better spot. But today the Maasai's way of life is in danger. Much of the Maasai's land has been taken away and turned into farms. Fences keep their herds from moving freely.

A Maasai man tends his flock of sheep on Kenya's savanna.

Maasai child

People Change Grasslands

Just as the Maasai struggle to keep their home, grasslands struggle against the effects people have on the land. South of Africa's Sahara desert lies the Sahel, a huge area of short grasses and bushes. Over the last 50 years, large parts of the Sahel have become deserts.

Over time, people have changed the landscape of the Sahel.

People are a main cause of this change. Bushes and trees were cut down for firewood. Farmers cleared grasses to plant crops. Without grasses to hold down the soil, winds blew sand and dirt from the Sahara across the Sahel. The Sahel became smaller as more and more sand kept grasses from growing.

Prairies once covered central North America. Today, only small areas of wild prairies are left. Prairie grasses were destroyed to make room for crops and ranches.

Protecting Grasslands

People have taken steps to protect grasslands. Governments set aside areas called preserves. Inside a **preserve**, native grassland plants and animals live in safety. The United States' Tallgrass Prairie National Preserve in Kansas protects one of the last stands of American prairies.

bee on butterfly weed flowers

In Minnesota, some farmers save wild prairie land on their farms. These protected fields become habitats for native plants and animals.

For thousands of years, people have used the rich soil of grasslands. They graze their cattle on them and cover the land with their homes. Now, people must work to save grasslands so they can survive for years to come.

Some farmers leave areas of their land alone so grasses and wildflowers can grow there.

CHAPTER 5

Grasslands Field Guide

Where to find grasslands:

Tropical grasslands grow in the warm areas of Africa, Asia, Australia, and South America. Temperate grasslands are found in Asia, Australia, Europe, North America, and South America.

CLIMATE:

Prairies receive 20 to 35 inches (51 to 89 centimeters) of rain each year. Savannas receive 20 to 50 inches (51 to 127 centimeters) of rain each year.

INSECTS:

many species including bumblebees, butterflies, black ants, grasshoppers, tiger moths

Questions:

How might you catch and study a grasshopper? Where would you look to find one?

ANIMALS:

- **Savanna animals:** cheetahs, elephants, gazelles, hyenas, lions, lizards, meerkats, zebras

- **Prairie animals:** black-footed ferrets, coyotes, deer, eagles, foxes, frogs, garter snakes, hawks, prairie dogs, skink lizards, turtles

PLANTS:

- **Savanna plants:** acacia trees, baobab trees, bermuda grasses, elephant grasses, lemon grasses

- **Prairie plants:** asters, big bluestem grasses, blazing stars, clover, coneflowers, cord grasses, grama grasses, Indian grasses, sunflowers, wild indigos

CHAPTER 6

A Scientist at Work

On northern Arizona's short-grass prairies, Dr. Con Slobodchikoff listens to prairie dogs. At the edge of a flat, grassy field, Slobodchikoff uses a microphone, tape recorder, and video camera to record the calls of the brown rodents. The small animals are on the lookout for danger. A prairie dog barks a loud warning when it spots a predator like a hawk.

After spending the day recording prairie dog sounds, Slobodchikoff takes his tapes back to his lab at Northern Arizona University. He uses a computer to study the sounds. Slobodchikoff has discovered more than 100 prairie dog words, including sounds for hawks, people, coyotes, and dogs. Slobodchikoff believes if animals like the prairie dog can think and communicate, then people should be more careful about how they treat animals and the places where they live.

GLOSSARY

biome (BUY-ome)—an area with a particular type of climate, and certain plants and animals that live there

climate (KLYE-mit)—the usual weather in a place

nectar (NEK-tur)—a sweet liquid that some insects collect from flowers and eat as food

predator (PRED-uh-tur)—an animal that hunts and eats other animals

preserve (pri-ZURV)—an area of land set aside by the government for a special purpose, such as protecting plants and animals

prey (PRAY)—an animal hunted by another animal

INTERNET SITES

FactHound offers a safe, fun way to find Internet sites related to this book. All of the sites on FactHound have been researched by our staff.

Here's how:

1. Visit *www.facthound.com*

2. Choose your grade level.

3. Type in this book ID **0736864059** for age-appropriate sites. You may also browse subjects by clicking on letters, or by clicking on pictures and words.

4. Click on the **Fetch It** button.

FactHound will fetch the best sites for you!

READ MORE

Johansson, Philip. *The Wide Open Grasslands: A Web of Life.* A World of Biomes. Berkeley Heights, N.J.: Enslow, 2004.

Reid, Greg. *Grasslands.* Ecosystems. Philadelphia: Chelsea Clubhouse, 2004.

Sievert, Terri. *Prairie Plants.* Life in the World's Biomes. Mankato, Minn.: Capstone Press, 2006.

INDEX

ABOUT THE AUTHOR

Kay Jackson

Kay Jackson writes nonfiction books for children. Kay has lived on and near North America's prairies. She's built snowmen on the short-grass prairies of New Mexico, picked flowers in the mixed grasses of Colorado, and camped among the tall grasses of northern Oklahoma. Kay lives and writes in Tulsa, Oklahoma, close to the last bit of North America's tallgrass prairie.